Trademarks: Goggles™ First Bear To Fly® Wright Bears™ Bearplane™

ISBN 978-0-473-50013-9

Aa

A is for airplane, flying way up high

Bb
B is for balloon,
floating in the sky

Cc

C is for clouds, gliding by the moon

Dd

**D is for drum,
going boom,
boom, boom!**

Ee
E is for elephant, strolling through the trees

Ff

F is for flag, waving in the breeze

Gg
G is for Grandpa,
resting tired feet

Hh
H is for honey, which bears love to eat

Ii
I is for ice cream, melting, pink and sweet

Jj
J is for jello,
a wobbly, yummy
treat

K k

K is for kite,
flying high and
free

L is for leaf,
falling from a tree

Mm
M is for mouse, who loves to nibble cheese

Nn

N is for nest, high up in the trees

Oo

O is for orange, juicy, fat and round

Pp

P is for propeller, makes a whizzing sound

Q
q
Q is for queen,
eating honey pie

Rr R is for rocket,
flying in the sky

S s

S is for sailboat,
on a starry night

Tt

T is for tortoise, with a **warning** light

U u
U is for umbrella,
keeps the rain
away

Vv
V is for violin,
which bears
love to play

Ww
W is for wand,
that casts a
magic spell

X is for xylophone,
chiming like
a bell

Yy
Y is for yellow
flowers, on a
sunny day

Zz

Z is for zoom, as the Wright Bears fly away!

A B C D E
F G H I J
K L M
N O P
Q R S T U
V W X Y Z

a b c d e
f g h i j
k l m n o
p q r s t
u v w
x y z

If you enjoyed the ABC, you'll love my 'Goggles' flying bear picture books.

Inspiring kids' imagination to take flight!

Jonathan Gunson - Author

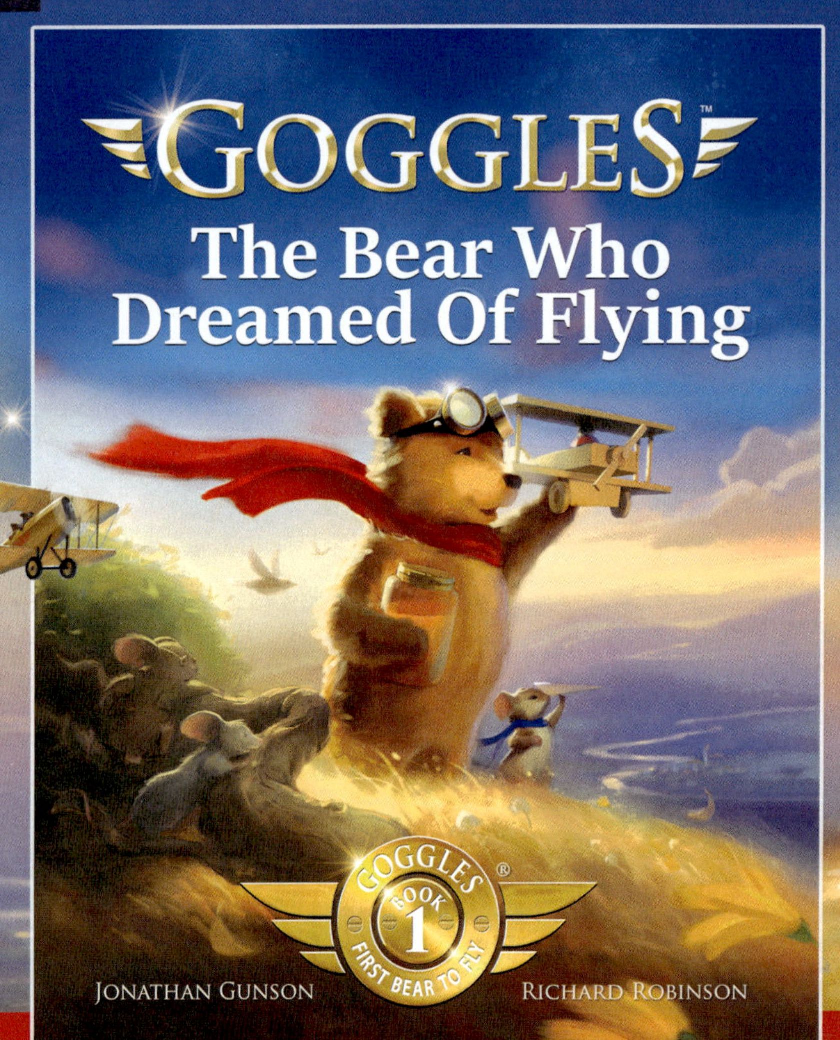

A Little Bear's Dream Of Flying Comes True

Goggles is a very small bear who dreams of flying. Everyone says he's too little, but one day he discovers a BIG SECRET that makes his dream come true.

Made in the USA
Monee, IL
23 February 2021